W9-BAS-903

PUBLIC LIBRARY
DISTRICT OF COLUMBIA

First Facts™

Holidays and Culture

Christmas

Season of Peace and Joy

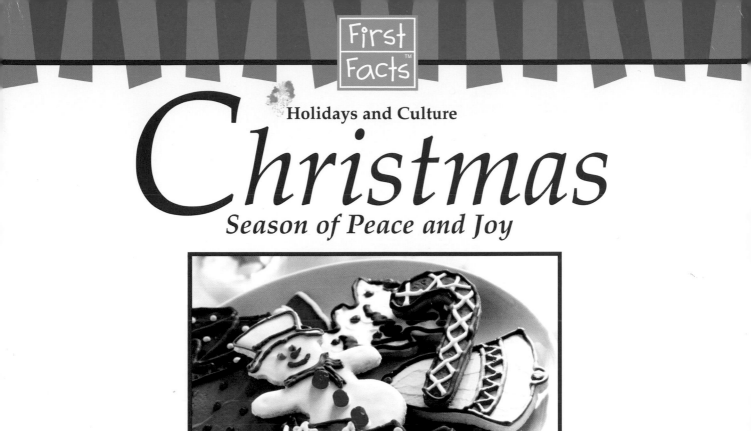

by Dori Hillestad Butler

Consultant:
David G. Hunter
Professor of Religious Studies, Iowa State University
Ames, Iowa

Capstone
press®
Mankato, Minnesota

First Facts is published by Capstone Press,
151 Good Counsel Drive, P.O. Box 669, Mankato, Minnesota 56002.
www.capstonepress.com

Copyright © 2007 by Capstone Press. All rights reserved.
No part of this publication may be reproduced in whole or in part, or stored in a retrieval system,
or transmitted in any form or by any means, electronic, mechanical, photocopying, recording, or
otherwise, without written permission of the publisher.
For information regarding permission, write to Capstone Press,
151 Good Counsel Drive, P.O. Box 669, Dept. R, Mankato, Minnesota 56002.
Printed in the United States of America

Library of Congress Cataloging-in-Publication Data
Butler, Dori Hillestad.
    Christmas : season of peace and joy / by Dori Hillestad Butler.
    p. cm.—(First facts. Holidays and culture)
    Summary: "Describes the history and meaning of Christmas and how it is celebrated today"—
Provided by publisher.
    Includes bibliographical references and index.
    ISBN-13: 978-0-7368-6394-0 (hardcover)
    ISBN-10: 0-7368-6394-X (hardcover)
    1. Christmas. 2. Jesus Christ—Nativity. I. Title. II. Series.
GT4985.B883 2007
394.2663—dc22   2006002827

Editorial Credits
Shari Joffe, editor; Biner Design, designer; Juliette Peters, set designer; Jo Miller, photo researcher;
    Scott Thoms, photo editor

Photo Credits
Capstone Press/Karon Dubke, 21
Corbis/Ariel Skelley, 4–5, 7; Bettmann, 8–9; K.M. Westermann, 6; Lew Robertson,
    cover; Reuters/Handout, 18; Star Ledger/Robert Sciarrino, 15
Getty Images Inc./The Image Bank/Rita Maas, 1; Time & Life Pictures/Mansell/Mansell, 20
PhotoEdit Inc./Myrleen Ferguson Cate, 14
Superstock/age fotostock, 12
The Granger Collection, New York, 11, 17
UNICORN Stock Photos/Robin Rudd, 19

1 2 3 4 5 6 11 10 09 08 07 06

Table of Contents

Celebrating Christmas 4

What Is Christmas? 6

Ancient Traditions 8

The Birth of Jesus 10

Christmas Trees 13

Giving 14

Santa Claus 16

Christmas Cards 18

Amazing Holiday Story! 20

Hands On: Outdoor Ornament 21

Glossary 22

Read More 23

Internet Sites 23

Index 24

Celebrating Christmas

Colorful lights twinkle on the tree. **Carols** like "Jingle Bells" and "Silent Night" play on the radio. Families and friends exchange presents, have a big meal, and wish each other "Merry Christmas." Many people look forward to Christmas all year long.

What Is Christmas?

Christians celebrate Christmas on December 25. On that day, they honor the birth of Jesus. Jesus lived 2,000 years ago. Christians believe he was the Son of God.

Families have their own Christmas
traditions. They may go to church,
decorate their homes, exchange gifts, or
make special foods.

Ancient Traditions

Many of today's Christmas traditions began long before Jesus was born. Back then, people held festivals during the dark days of winter to welcome back the sun. Feasts, gifts, and caroling were part of some of these festivals.

Fact!

Over time, as people became Christian, their winter festival traditions blended with celebrations of Jesus' birth.

9

The Birth of Jesus

The Bible tells the story of Jesus' birth. Mary and Joseph came to Bethlehem after a long journey. The inn had no rooms, so they slept in a stable. There, Jesus was born.

An angel told nearby **shepherds** that a **savior** was born. A great star appeared. It led three wise men to Jesus. The wise men gave Jesus gifts and spread the news of his birth.

Fact!

No one knows the date of Jesus' birth. In the 300s, Pope Julius I decided it should be celebrated on December 25.

11

Christmas Trees

In the 1500s, German families started bringing evergreen trees into their homes during the holiday season. These trees were called "Christ trees." People decorated them with fruits, candies, and cookies. Some even put candles on the branches. Today people use lights rather than candles. They may also put ornaments and tinsel on their Christmas trees.

Fact!

The star on top of many people's Christmas trees is a reminder of the star of Bethlehem.

Giving

Families give each other gifts on Christmas Eve or Christmas morning. This tradition is a reminder of the wise mens' gifts to Jesus.

Christmas is also a time to give to those in need. People may collect clothing, toys, food, or money to help the poor.

Santa Claus

Many children believe that if they are good, St. Nicholas, or Santa Claus, will bring them gifts on Christmas.

There really was a St. Nicholas. He was a **bishop** who lived in the fourth century. He loved children and gave gifts to the poor. Today Santa Claus is a **symbol** of the kindness and giving that are part of celebrating Christmas.

Fact!

The name Santa Claus comes from *Sinterklaas*, the Dutch nickname for St. Nicholas.

17

Christmas Cards

In 1843, a man named Henry Cole was too busy to write Christmas greetings. He hired artist John Horsley to design the first Christmas card.

Today, many people mail Christmas cards to friends and family. These cards send good wishes during this special time of caring and giving.

Amazing Holiday Story!

In 1914, Germany was at war with Great Britain and France. But on Christmas Eve, German troops sang carols and decorated trees outside their trenches. They put up signs that read, "We no fight, you no fight." The other side agreed. Soldiers from both sides came out of the trenches and exchanged gifts. Some even played a game of soccer. For one day, in the midst of war, there truly was peace on Earth.

Hands On:
Outdoor Ornament

People usually decorate their indoor Christmas trees with beautiful ornaments. Try making this outdoor Christmas tree ornament for birds to enjoy!

What You Need

1 large pinecone with stem
$1/2$ cup (120 mL) cornmeal
$1/2$ cup (120 mL) solid vegetable shortening or lard
medium-sized mixing bowl

birdseed
shallow dish
string
scissors

What You Do

1. Use the scissors to cut a piece of string about 10 inches (25.4 centimeters) long.
2. Tie the string into a loop. Then tie the loop to the end of the pinecone.
3. In the bowl, mix the cornmeal with the shortening or lard.
4. Roll the pinecone in the mixture.
5. Pour birdseed into the shallow dish.
6. Roll the pinecone in the birdseed.
7. Hang your finished ornament on your favorite tree outside.

Glossary

bishop (BISH-uhp)—a senior priest in the Catholic church

carol (KAR-ruhl)—joyful song sung at Christmastime

Christian (KRISS-chin)—a person who follows a religion based on the teachings of Jesus

savior (SAYV-yuhr)—a person who arrives to save people

shepherd (SHEP-urd)—a person whose job it is to look after sheep

symbol (SIM-buhl)—a design or an object that stands for something else

tradition (truh-DISH-uhn)—a custom, idea, or belief passed down through time

Read More

Foran, Jill. *Christmas.* Celebrating Cultures. Mankato, Minn.: Weigl Publishers, 2003.

Haugen, Brenda. *Christmas.* Holidays and Celebrations. Minneapolis: Picture Window Books, 2004.

Houghton, Gillian. *Christmas.* My Library of Holidays. New York: PowerKids Press, 2004.

Internet Sites

FactHound offers a safe, fun way to find Internet sites related to this book. All of the sites on FactHound have been researched by our staff.

Here's how:

1. Visit *www.facthound.com*

2. Choose your grade level.

3. Type in this book ID 073686394X for age-appropriate sites. You may also browse subjects by clicking on letters, or by clicking on pictures and words.

4. Click on the **Fetch It** button.

FactHound will fetch the best sites for you!

Index

angel, 10

Bethlehem, 10, 13
Bible, the, 10
birth of Jesus, 10

candles, 13
cards, 18–19
carols, 4, 8, 20
Christians, 6
Christmas Eve, 14, 20
Christmas morning, 14
church, 7
Cole, Henry, 18
cookies, 13

families, 4, 7, 13, 14, 19
feasts, 8
food, 4, 7
friends, 4, 19

gifts, 4, 7, 10, 14, 15, 16, 20
giving, 14–15, 16, 19

Horsley, John, 18

Jesus, 6, 8, 10
Joseph, 10

lights, 4, 13

Mary, 10

ornaments, 13

Pope Julius I, 10
presents. See gifts

Santa Claus, 16
savior, 10
shepherds, 10
star, 10, 13
St. Nicholas, 16

tinsel, 13
traditions, 7, 8
trees, 4, 13, 20

winter festivals, 8
wise men, 10, 14